If I Were A...
BALLERINA
The world of ballet in pictures!

NorthParadePublishing

Published in 2011 by North Parade Publishing Ltd.
4 North Parade
Bath
BA1 1LF
UK

If I Were A...
BALLERINA
The world of ballet in pictures!

INTRODUCTION

Welcome to the magical world of ballet! In this book you'll experience this classical and popular dance form in a whole new way—by seeing an array of pictures and reading about it at the same time. This book is a pictorial insight into the world of the ballet dancer.

An easy read book designed to acquaint children with the various moves and activities that the typical ballet dancer has to undertake in order to be successful.

In ballet you have to move your hands and feet in just the right manner. The movements might look easy, but are pretty tough to master. It takes a lot of practice.

Dancers wear special shoes or slippers. These slippers are very flexible and have thin soles. They help the dancer perform the difficult moves.

One of the things dancers have to learn is to perform "en pointe", which is how to dance on the tips of their toes. It can be very difficult.

Footwork is very important in ballet dancing. You have to develop great lower body strength to be able to accomplish the beautiful moves.

A ballet dancer's body has to be flexible. Dancers have to perform special exercises. Stretching is an important part of a dancer's routine.

Always check with a
trained ballet teacher or
parent on what stretching
exercises are safe for you
to do and when.

Another very difficult move to master in ballet is the split. Splits are named according to whichever foot is extended in front.

It is extremely important to be strong and limber to perform the intricate movements of ballet. Performing amazing leaps and jumps can take years of practice.

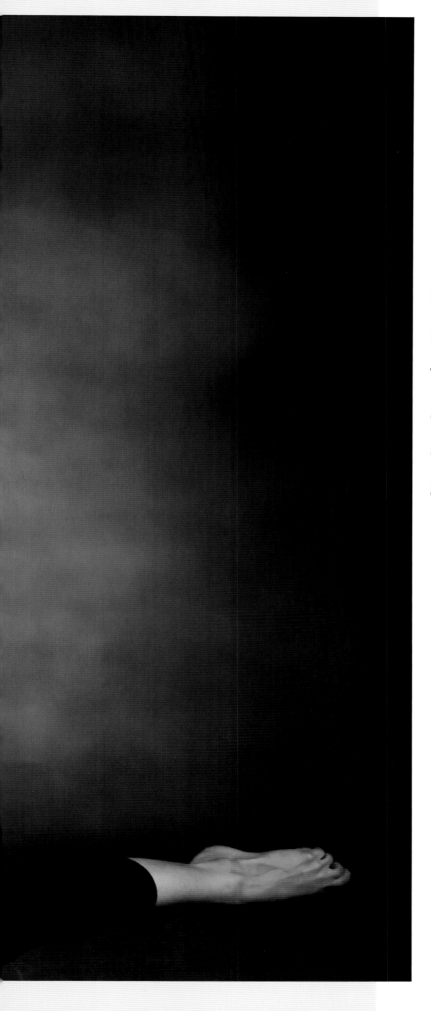

Once you have learnt
a few steps, it will be
fun trying them out with
accompanying music.
See if you can create
a routine!

The ballet barre is a handrail that is mainly used by dancers to perform warm up exercises. Barres can be made of metal, wood or both.

If you have already created a routine that you like to perform to a piece of music, maybe it's time to decide on a striking final pose. End with a flourish!

Choreographers often design routines where the ballet dancers seem to do impossible things. Some dancers look like they can fly.

Ballerinas wear special dresses when performing. See the ruffled, fluffy skirts? These are called tutus. They come in a variety of colours like pink, white, blue, etc.

Striking compositions can be achieved by chorus groups. All the dancers execute their movements together and with perfection. This gives the dance a dazzling effect.

In ballet school, you will be taught the precise methods and techniques for different steps. Follow your instructor carefully and be careful to avoid injury.

Ballet incorporates movements that are known as pliés and pirouettes. After years of training dancers can perform some really amazing movements.

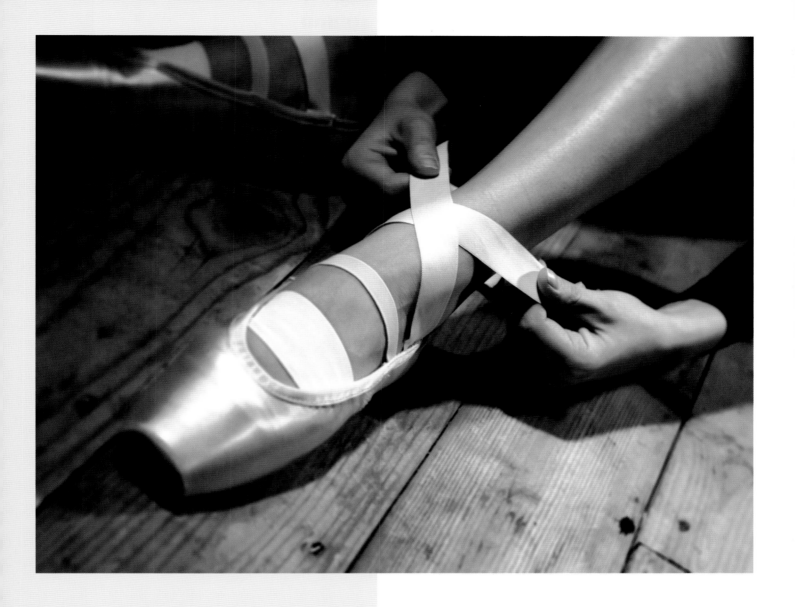

When you begin learning to dance, you will probably start by using ballet shoes. Later you will be allowed to wear pointe shoes. These have a flat front end to protect the dancer's toes.

You may need to train for five years or more to go from ballet shoes to pointe shoes.

There are five basic positions in ballet that you will have to master first. These will be the foundation to learning more complicated moves.

Many methods in ballet are named after their originators. There is the Vaganova method and the Legat method to name a few.

Any jump in ballet requires a strong back and legs and requires focus, timing and fitness.

Ballet dancers tend to be fussy about their feet as they are the tools of their trade!

Dancing in the ballet takes many hours of practice. To make it to the top of this profession takes time and absolute dedication.

A group performance means that every member in the group has to be totally attuned to the others in the group so that every move is synchronised.

Even when only two people are dancing, there has to be perfect co-ordination between them so the dance appears smooth and flawless.

Every member in the
group has to strike the
same pose with the limbs
held in the exact same
position. Otherwise the
setup will look awkward.

Every movement in ballet conveys a world of emotion. No wonder, this dance form is considered one of the most dramatic dance forms in the world.

But ballet is not just
about the dance moves.
Every ballet must have
the right costume and
makeup, otherwise the
performance will fall flat.

GLOSSARY

Attuned: receptive or aware; harmonious

Ballerina: a female ballet dancer

Ballet: a form of classical dance with formalised steps and gestures set in complex patterns

Barre: a handrail placed at hip height, used by a dancer to maintain balance during practice

Composition: the arrangement of individual dance steps to form a complete movement

En pointe: a position in ballet where the dancer has to stand on the tips of her toes

Flawless: a dance movement that does not have any defects or mistakes

Flourish: a dramatic and sweeping gesture

Legat method: a system of ballet developed by the Russian ballet dancer Nikolai Legat

Limber: easily able to bend the limbs

Pirouette: whirling about on one foot or on the points of the toes

Plié: a ballet movement in which the knees are bent while the back is held straight

Regimen: a regulated system of exercise

Routine: a performance, or part of it, given regularly by a dancer

Splits: the act of separating the legs while sinking to the floor, until they extend at right angles to the body

Synchronised: in dancing, to move at the same rate and exactly together